IMAGES OF THE NEW FOREST

THE LANDSCAPE AND VILLAGES

SALMON

Front cover: Ponies in Bolderwood
Back cover: Dockens Water, Digden Bottom
Title page: Swan Green, Lyndhurst
This page: Golden colours of autumn

This unique corner of England was set aside more than nine hundred years ago by William the Conqueror, who named it his "New" forest. Here the vast acres of woodland and heath were to be protected to enable royal hunting parties to enjoy the thrill of the chase in pursuit of deer and other wild quarry. This royal protection has bequeathed a landscape which is little changed since medieval times, where ancient oak and beech woodland mingle with streams and open wilderness, and where deer and ponies graze in freedom.

Despite its name, in fact less than half of the Forest's 150 or so square miles is wooded. The remainder comprises heather and bracken-clad heath, open pastureland and marshy ground. The actual forested areas are made up of the ancient woodland – mainly of mighty oaks and beeches – where the wildlife can roam freely, and the enclosures, fenced-off areas of coniferous or deciduous woodland given over to timber production. Interspersed throughout the forest are the thatched homesteads which typify the area, and the larger settlements like Lyndhurst, Brockenhurst and Burley, which now provide excellent centres from which to explore either by car or on foot, by bicycle or on horseback, into the deeper recesses of the woods.

The ancient traditions and atmosphere of the Forest are preserved by a system of Verderers, Agisters and Keepers, forest officials whose origins date back to medieval times and who are responsible for management of the ponies and wildlife, for protecting the common rights of the forest inhabitants and for conservation of the woodland and the natural environment.

Today, despite its proximity to Southampton and Bournemouth and the tourist coastlines of Dorset and Hampshire, the New Forest has retained a timeless feel quite unlike any other part of England. Here it is possible to escape the rush of modern life, to experience a closeness to nature and a rich variety of wildlife and to enjoy the moods of a landscape whose atmosphere is ever-changing from dawn to dusk and from season to season.

Situated on the northern edge of the forest, Bramshaw is a pretty, if somewhat straggling, village. It consists largely of farms and smallholdings scattered among the trees, and the interesting old church stands on a hillock surrounded by rhododendrons. In springtime, Bramshaw Woods bursts into life, and mosses and fungi carpet the woodland floor.

Evening sunshine filters through the trees in the Rhinefield Enclosure, situated in the heart of the forest. The nearby Ornamental Drive is lined with colourful flowering shrubs, including azaleas and rhododendrons, set against a backdrop of firs, cedars and sequoias.

Evening sunshine throws long shadows, and the ancient beech trees of Bramshaw Woods glow in the golden light of autumn.

Situated on the north-western extremity of the New Forest, Rockford Common lies in one of the least frequented parts of this delightful region. In autumn the bracken-covered slopes are transformed into a rich golden carpet.

Comprising ancient woods of oak, beech, holly and yew, the forest also has fenced plantations of conifers grown for their timber. At Mogshade Hill near Minstead, calm descends over the countryside at the end of a winter's day, and the ancient woodland takes on a mysterious brooding quality.

Typical of the 16,000 acres of Forestry Commission enclosures is Milkham Enclosure near Linwood, where shafts of autumn sunlight filter through the trees and fall on the golden fronds of bracken below.

The first rays of pale morning sunshine highlight the purple heather blooms on Rockford Common.

Dawn rises over Fritham in a remote northern part of the New Forest, an ancient area full of atmosphere where fossils and Roman remains have been found. There are extensive views from Fritham northwards to Salisbury, and south-west across the Avon valley.

Numerous streams and rivulets thread their way through the forest, providing an ideal habitat for a rich variety of wild life. Little Dockens Water meanders through a sun-dappled glade at Digden Bottom near Linwood.

The gnarled branches of these magnificent beech trees spread a canopy above the ground in Mark Ash Wood, the largest beechwood in the forest.

Every part of the New Forest has its own unique beauty, and from the wild heights of Stoney Cross Plain there are panoramic views of the bracken-filled hollows, wooded valleys and open moorland which stretch away into the distance.

The River Avon forms the western boundary of the New Forest and from Castle Hill, near the attractive hamlet of Godshill, there are some magnificent views extending across a large part of the tranquil Avon valley.

HERE STOOD
THE OAK TREE,
ON WHICH AN ARROW
SHOT BY
SIR WALTER TYRRELL
AT A STAG,
GLANCED AND STRUCK
KING WILLIAM
THE SECOND,
SURNAMED RUFUS,
ON THE BREAST,
OF WHICH HE
INSTANTLY DIED,
ON THE SECOND
DAY OF AUGUST,
ANNO 1100.

Frost lingers beneath the trees around the Rufus Stone, the legendary site of the death, in 1100, of King William II. The king, who was known as William Rufus, was shot by an arrow while hunting deer in the forest, but whether by accident or intent has never been proved.

The northern expanses of the New Forest are the highest and least visited part of this popular area, characterised by bracken-filled glades and shady enclosures. Puckpitts Enclosure near Minstead was once a haunt of badgers and buzzards, but both are less numerous today than they once were.

A timeless scene is revealed at Half Moon Common near Wellow as the early mist clears from this ancient, marshy heathland with its encircling trees and clumps of autumn-tinted bracken.

Numerous footpaths meander across Bolderwood making the area, which encompasses many different types of woodland and gives shelter to both ponies and deer, a paradise for walkers.

East of Lyndhurst lie the vast heathlands of Matley and Yew Tree Heath, purple with heather and fringed with alder and birch trees. Looking towards Southampton Water, Stephill Bottom is seen here bathed in early light at sunrise. Just past quaintly named Pig Bush, on the road from Lyndhurst to Beaulieu, is Buck Hill. Here, where a thick belt of woodland crosses the vast expanse of Beaulieu Heath, there are lovely views.

The early morning mist begins to lift from the grassy heathland around Cadnam, an ancient village of some importance which lies
at the north-eastern edge of the forest. Here a group of ponies grazing close to the shelter of the trees creates a typical scene.

Although the ponies are the best known of all the animals that roam freely through the woods and moorland of the New Forest, a number of donkeys can also be seen grazing in secluded glades or by the roadside. Like the ponies, these sturdy animals live out in the open in all weathers.

The New Forest ponies, often seen grazing in secluded glades or by the roadside, are a great attraction with visitors. They are found in a wide range of colours from strawberry roan to dark brown. About 3000 of these small, hardy animals, belonging to a breed which may well go back to prehistoric times, live out in the open in all weathers. Although they may appear to be running wild, the ponies are all now owned by the New Forest Commoners, and once a year they are rounded up for branding and marking in spectacular autumn "drifts".

At Markway Bridge in the heart of the forest there are open expanses of grassy heathland where deer and ponies graze in the morning mist of early summer, close to the shelter of the trees.

Common rights for forest dwellers to graze their animals on forest land have existed for over 900 years. The ancient right to graze pigs on acorns, known as "pannage", is permitted mainly in the autumn.

Deer, descendants of animals hunted by William the Conqueror, are less plentiful than they used to be but can still be seen, especially at dawn or dusk when they are feeding. Of the four species found in the forest, the pretty fallow deer is the commonest.

Burley is an excellent centre for woodland walks or horse riding. Near the pretty little green with its stone cross stands the Queen's Head, an intriguing old inn which was once a haunt of smugglers and is probably the oldest house in this attractive village.

Presenting a typical New Forest scene, this splendid thatched cottage stands amidst fine woodland scenery at Swan Green on the outskirts of Lyndhurst. Here, too, wild ponies roam the lanes and graze by the roadside.

Known as the "Capital of the New Forest", Lyndhurst, which means lime woodland, is an attractive town of narrow streets and impressive Victorian and Edwardian architecture.

Situated in the heart of the New Forest, Brockenhurst is a charming village where ponies and cattle meander through the streets at will. The pretty little Brookley Watersplash crosses the main street, providing a natural watering place. The outstanding feature of this bustling village is the parish church, which is built of stone and brick and has a tower capped by a shingle spire. A massive yew tree said to be more than 1000 years old stands near the door, its branches spanning over seventy feet.

The dawn light of a winter's morning catches the squat tower of Boldre church, which dates from about 1130, although it has later additions and alterations. A past vicar of Boldre, William Gilpin, whose writings such as *Forest Sketches* brought him fame as a naturalist, is buried in the graveyard.

At nightfall the view down cobbled Quay Hill in Lymington presents a peaceful scene as lights come on in the shop windows.

The ancient town of Lymington once rivalled Portsmouth and Southampton as a major port, and boat building was carried on here for many centuries. Quay Hill, with its graceful Georgian and Victorian houses and shops, leads up from the tidal harbour and is a scene of activity when the 700-year-old market takes place.

Today, Lymington's sheltered harbour on the Lymington River is used less for commerce than for recreation. The busy Town Quay is a popular yachting centre, and the harbour is usually full to capacity with boats. The numerous creeks and inlets were much frequented by smugglers in the 17th and 18th centuries.

The peaceful hamlet of Bucklers Hard comprises two rows of cottages lining a single wide main street beside the lovely Beaulieu River. In the 18th century, it was a thriving shipbuilding community and many of England's "wooden walls" were built and launched at Bucklers Hard, including Nelson's *Agamemnon*.

As the sky begins to brighten and early morning mist rises off the river, reflections in the still waters of the Beaulieu River create a tranquil scene.

The great Cistercian abbey of Beaulieu, founded in 1204, has largely fallen into ruins. The monks' refectory is now used as the parish church and the original gatehouse, known as Palace House, has become the home of Lord Montagu of Beaulieu.

Exbury Gardens near Beaulieu are among the most outstanding gardens in the south-east of England. They provide something for every season but they are particularly spectacular during the late spring and summer when dramatic effects are created by the rhododendrons, camellias and roses.

Situated at the head of the Beaulieu River estuary, the unspoiled village of Beaulieu is made up of a cluster of red-brick cottages and a picturesque old inn. In spring, Palace House provides the backdrop to a carpet of golden daffodils.

The little Domesday village of Minstead, with its unusually named Trusty Servant Inn, lies in the northern part of the New Forest. The quaint, painted inn sign depicts a figure with a pig's head, donkey's ears, padlocked jaw and deer's feet, supposedly the qualities required of the ideal servant.

Azaleas, rhododendrons and many other flowering shrubs provide a stunning display of early summer colour in Furzey Gardens at Minstead. The thatched cottage in the grounds dates from 1560, and houses a collection of local arts and crafts.

Situated on the River Avon, the busy market town of Ringwood has an attractive, curving main street with a number of fine old buildings. This magnificent half-timbered inn with its snug thatched roof is typical of the ancient homesteads which are found throughout the forest.

Set in a hollow of the Hampshire Downs, the delightful village of Rockbourne comprises a harmonious mixture of building styles. Attractive 16th to 18th century houses line the main street where cottages with cob walls and thatched roofs stand side by side with brick and tile, or timber and stone.

The village of Breamore, three miles north of Fordingbridge, has been carefully preserved against change and development, and is one of the most beautiful villages in the forest. This fine timber, brick and thatch house is typical of the cottage architecture in this part of southern England.

Rhododendrons and azaleas provide a spectacular late spring display along the Ornamental Drive.

Printed and published by J. Salmon Ltd., Sevenoaks, Kent TN13 1BB

Designed by the Salmon Studio. Copyright © 2002 J. Salmon Ltd.

ISBN   1 902842 36 7

Stock Code   12-06-57-01